WRITING EXCITING SENTENCES:
Age 7 PLUS

Alan Peat

CREATIVE EDUCATIONAL PRESS LTD

PUBLISHED BY: Creative Educational Press Ltd
                       2 The Walled Garden
                       Grange Park Drive
                       Biddulph
                       Staffs
                       ST8 7TA

                       Tel: 07789938923
                       Fax: 01782 379398

PRINTED BY: York Publishing Services Ltd.,
                       64, Hallfield Road, Layerthorpe, York, YO31 7ZQ

DESIGN: Julie Peat

COVER DESIGN: Glyn and Simon Matthews

Alan Peat   www.alanpeat.com
                       info@alanpeat.com

Glyn Matthews   www.glyn-matthews.co.uk
                       info@glyn-matthews.co.uk

ISBN: 978-0-9544755-3-6

When stated, pages from this book may be photocopied for use by the purchaser or purchasing institution only. Otherwise all rights are reserved and text/illustrations may not be reprinted or reproduced or utilised in any form or by any electronic, mechanical or other means, now known or hereafter invented, including photocopying and recording, or in any information storage or retrieval system, without permission in writing from the publishers.

Also available from Creative Educational Press Ltd (www.thecepress.com):

A Second Book of Exciting Sentences by Alan Peat and Mathew Sullivan
50 Ways to Retell a Story: Cinderella by Alan Peat, Julie Peat and Christopher Storey
Get Your Head Around Punctuation (...and how to teach it!) by Alan Peat
The Elves and The Shoemaker 1897 illustrated by John Harrold
Writing Exciting Ghost Stories: Age 9 Plus: Ghost Story Plot Skeletons by Alan Peat
(co-author Julie Barnfather)
Teaching Outstanding Persuasive Writing by Alan Peat
Developing Writing Through Comics by Mathew Sullivan
The Magic Stone by Alan Peat (illustrated by John Harrold)
Word Warriors (CD-ROM Game) design by Simon Matthews
Spelling Bee (CD-ROM Game) design by Simon Matthews

ACKNOWLEDGEMENTS

Many thanks to:
Staff and pupils at Wyche CE Primary School, Malvern, especially Green class; Year Six teacher, Jon Westwood; pupils: Alice Kent, Matthew Chauhan, Sally Fitzpatrick, Katie Jackson-Read, Marcello Cossali-Francis, Cameron Lewis, Gillian Wight, Timmy Tedds, Joshua Brooks, Daniel Sillitoe, Jonah Pickering, Harry Davies, William Waite, Hatty Senior, Harry Senior, Kimberley Palmer, Bethany Williams, Edward Lowe and Hope Speight.
We hope you enjoy seeing 'your' book in print!
Head Teacher Sarah Thursfield, her staff and pupils at Christ Church CE Primary School, Fenton, Stoke on Trent.
And, as ever, grateful thanks to Literacy Coordinator Lyn Houston, staff and pupils at Anglesey Primary School, Lozells, Birmingham for their continued help and support.

ALAN PEAT

CONTENTS

TITLE		PAGE
1. BOYS (But Or, Yet and So)	sentences	11.
2. 2A (2 adjectives before/after the noun)	sentences	13.
3. SIMILE (like a …/ as a …)	sentences	15.
4. 3 ___ed (3 related adjectives)	sentences	17.
5. 2 pairs	sentences	19.
6. De:De (Description:Details)	sentences	21.
7. Verb, person	sentences	23.
8. O.(I.) (Outside/Inside)	sentences	25.
9. If, if, if, then	sentences	27.
10. Emotion word, comma	sentences	29.
11. NOUN, which/who/where	sentences	31.
12. MANY QUESTIONS	sentences	33.
13. Ad, same ad	sentences	35.
14. 3 bad—(dash) question?	sentences	37.
15. Double ly ending	sentences	39.
16. All the W's	sentences	41.
17. LIST	sentences	43.
18. Some; others	sentences	45.
19. Personification of weather	sentences	47.
20. P.C.	sentences	49.
21. The more, the more	sentences	51.
22. SHORT	sentences	53.
23. ___ing, ___ed	sentences	55.
24. Irony	sentences	57.
25. IMAGINE 3 examples:	sentences	59.
APPENDIX 1 - Colour coded display and target setting		61.
APPENDIX 2 - Using a broad range of Connectives: Physical Reminders		63.
APPENDIX 3 — Jon Westwood, Wyche Primary School		65.

Introduction

The ability to produce effective sentences is one of the cornerstones of a well-crafted piece of writing. Many pupils already know how to write simple sentences. This book will help pupils to write more varied sentences which engage and captivate the reader.

What is a sentence?

A sentence is a written or spoken means of communicating an idea or series of ideas. Other than the one word sentence, a sentence is a group of words that makes sense on its own. It *must* have a verb, it *must* start with a capital letter and it *must* end with a full stop, exclamation mark or question mark. Normally sentences contain one or more subject-verb combinations.
Pupils should also be taught that a sentence can be made up of only one word. The following are examples of one word sentences:

A. *"What?"*
B. *"Ouch!"*
C. *"Run!"*

The single-word sentence communicates a whole idea which is understood by the reader/listener, for example:

1. *"What?"* could be a shortened form of "What did you say?"

2. *"Ouch!"* effectively communicates 'something hurt me' in a shortened manner.

3. *"Run!"* is clearly a command and the brevity suggests urgency.

Most sentences are, however, more than one word long. The typical teaching sequence for sentences begins with the simple *subject/verb* sentence, for example:

SUBJECT	VERB
Dogs	*bark.*

This is usually extended by adding adjectives to the subject and/or verbs:

ADJECTIVE	*SUBJECT*	*VERB*
Large	*dogs*	*bark.*

Beyond simple sentences

Many pupils develop longer sentences through imitation, particularly of sentences which they read or hear spoken.

When pupils have grasped the *subject/verb* sentence form, how do we help them to expand their range of sentence types?

The issue is one of clarity and it is my belief that the complex vocabulary, often used to describe the structure of extended sentences, can alienate pupils who might otherwise become enthusiastic writers.

Although the teacher may be interested in distinguishing between compound, complex and compound complex sentences, I have rarely met a primary aged pupil who is gripped by such an exercise. Likewise, prepositional phrases, participial phrases and infinitive phrases *leave me cold*, yet I love writing. Writing is a pleasurable, everyday part of my life. I'm sure I am not alone in thinking this and although I know that meta-language is a necessary part of any subject, I don't want the 'language of language' to become a barrier to pupils' enjoyment of writing.

Keep it simple:make it stick

Throughout this booklet I have tried to simplify the complex language often used to describe sentences and sentence structures. This does not make the book simplistic, but rather it makes it deliberately simple: simple with the end aim being that the greatest number of pupils are able to write the broadest range of sentence types.

With this in mind, I have given each sentence an easy-to-remember name. This has proved successful in my own teaching. An example will clarify this: instead of asking for a sentence with a coordinating conjunction (which wouldn't work with the majority of pupils I have taught!) I ask for a *BOYS* sentence—*BOYS* being a mnemonic for:

> But, Or, Yet, So

If pupils write sentences which include one of these words, then they will undoubtedly have produced a sentence with a coordinating conjunction—it's just that the simple mnemonic makes it more achievable and memorable. It also provides an easy self-assessment mechanism: "Have I remembered some BOYS sentences?"

How to use this booklet

Twenty five different sentence types are described in the booklet. They are in no particular order and all have been used, successfully, with pupils aged between seven and fourteen. Each sentence type is given a title, which should be used regularly with pupils, as it is one of the keys to remembering the sentence type. This is followed by some examples for class use, a brief explanation of the sentence type and a range of teaching 'tips' which have worked for me and other teachers who have piloted the approach.

It is hoped that all of these sentence types will be taught in the context of writing activities designed to engage and motivate pupils. It should be obvious that isolated 'drilling' of these sentence types could be as off-putting for a pupil as a worksheet.

The range included is by no means exhaustive, but if used in the manner suggested, it should help pupils to use a varied range of sentence types at appropriate points in both their fiction and non-fiction writing. Once they have been explained, modelled and used in the classroom, pupils may begin to identify examples of these sentence types in the work of authors they read. They should be encouraged to collect these examples, which can be used to create a useful visual display showing pupils the various sentence types used in the context of effective, exciting writing.

As one pupil from Anglesey Primary School, Birmingham observed when reading *Harry Potter*:

"J.K. Rowling must have used all of these!"

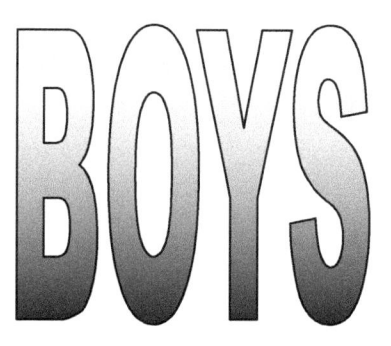

1. TITLE: BOYS SENTENCES

EXAMPLES:

a.   He was a friendly man most of the time, <u>but</u> he could become nasty.

b.   He could be really friendly, <u>or</u> he could be miserable.

c.   It was a warm day, <u>yet</u> storm clouds gathered over the distant mountains.

d.   It was a beautiful morning for a walk, <u>so</u> he set off quite happily.

EXPLANATION:

A BOYS sentence is basically a two-part sentence. The first part of the sentence always ends with a comma and the latter part always begins with a coordinating conjunction. The most popular coordinating conjunctions are:

<u>B</u>ut, <u>O</u>r, <u>Y</u>et (and) <u>S</u>o

the first letters of which provide the mnemonic : *BOYS*

TEACHING TIPS:

Model how to turn two separate sentences into BOYS sentences -

It was a beautiful morning for a walk. He set off happily.

becomes

It was a beautiful morning for a walk, so he set off happily.

To achieve this, stress the need to turn the full-stop into a comma and follow the comma with one of the coordinating conjunctions (BOYS words).

2. TITLE: 2A SENTENCES

EXAMPLES:

a. He was a tall, awkward man with an old, crumpled jacket.
       ⇩   ⇩   ⬇   ⇩   ⇩   ⬇
   adj 1 adj 2 1st noun   adj 3 adj 4 2nd noun

b. It was an overgrown, messy garden with a lifeless, leafless tree.
         ⇩   ⇩   ⬇   ⇩   ⇩   ⬇
    adj 1   adj 2 1st noun   adj 3 adj4 2nd noun

EXPLANATION:

A 2A sentence has two adjectives preceding the first noun, followed by a further two adjectives preceding a second noun. This type of sentence is particularly useful as a way of creating a strong visual image in the reader's mind. It helps pupils to produce more descriptive writing.

TEACHING TIPS:

When teaching 2A sentences, attention should be drawn to the comma separating the first two adjectives and the comma separating the second two adjectives.
The teacher may also wish to introduce alliteration (patterned use of language) as in example b above: *... lifeless, leafless ...*
If alliteration is introduced it is often wise to set an upper limit, for example: *"Remember, no more than two examples of alliteration in a story."*
Note also how, in example b, only two of the adjectives (rather than all four) alliterate.
I always set the 'rule' that only two adjectives in any one sentence alliterate.
Four alliterating adjectives always appear excessive!!!

3. TITLE: SIMILE ... like a ... ... as a ... SENTENCES

EXAMPLES:

a. The moon hung above us <u>like a</u> patient, pale white face.

b. Although it was August it was as cold <u>as a</u> late December evening.

EXPLANATION:

A *simile sentence* has, quite obviously, a central simile which creates a vivid picture in the reader's mind.

With younger pupils, I call these ... *like a* ... and ... *as a* ... sentences as this provides the writer with the language of comparison necessary when creating similes.

TEACHING TIPS:

The key to producing an effective *simile sentence* is to avoid cliché. One way of achieving this is to start by producing a poster of *Banned Similes* such as;

BANNED

It was as cold as ice.

It was as hot as the sun.

He shivered like a leaf.

I then show children a method of making such banned similes more interesting by adding 'Where?' and 'When?' to the end of the cliché, for example

BANNED
It was as cold as ice.

becomes

BETTER

It was as cold as ice <u>floating in the Arctic ocean</u> on a <u>moonlit winter night.</u>

⇩ ⇩

WHERE? **WHEN?**
(Think of a very cold place) **(Think of a time when it is very cold)**

4. TITLE: 3 ___ed SENTENCES

EXAMPLES:

a. Frighten**ed**, terrifi**ed**, exhaust**ed**, they ran from the creature.

b. Amus**ed**, amaz**ed**, excit**ed**, he left the circus reluctantly.

c. Confus**ed**, troubl**ed**, worri**ed**, she didn't know what had happened.

EXPLANATION:

A *3___ed* sentence begins with three related adjectives, each of which ends in ___ed. All 3 ___ed words must be followed by commas. Most ___ed words used to open this sentence type describe emotions e.g.

Horrifi**ed**
Amus**ed**
Confus**ed**

3___ed sentences are therefore particularly useful when the writer is accentuating a character's emotions.

TEACHING TIPS:

For less able pupils a *2___ed* sentence is still effective. The difficulty is always one of finding sufficient *ED* words for pupils to use! I display a poster in class with a broad range of alpha-ordered adjectives ending in ___ed.

Pupils are encouraged to add to the poster when they find other examples. This could also be linked to pupils' use of a Thesaurus in the classroom.

An alpha-ordered list is included below:

A	Amused, Angered, Amazed, Appreciated
B	Bored, Bemused, Bewildered, Bothered
C	Confused, Controlled,
D	Disappointed, Dejected
E	Excited, Elated
F	Frightened, Feared
G	Gladdened, Guarded
H	Horrified, Hated
I	Interested, Introverted, Intrigued
J	Jaded
K	Kissed
L	Loved, Loathed, Liked
M	Maddened, Mellowed
N	Numbed, Nurtured
O	Overawed
P	Perplexed, Perturbed
Q	Quietened, Questioned
R	Relaxed, Relieved
S	Shocked, Startled
T	Terrified, Troubled
U	Unnerved, Uninterested
V	Vexed, Valued
W	Worried, Wretched
X	
Y	
Z	Zonked

5. TITLE: **2 pairs** SENTENCES

EXAMPLES:

a. Exhausted and worried, cold and hungry, they did not know how much further they had to go.

b. Injured and terrified, shell-shocked and lost, he wandered aimlessly across the battlefield.

c. Angry and bewildered, numb and fearful, he couldn't believe that this was happening to him.

EXPLANATION:

Dramatic in its succinctness, a *2 pairs* sentence begins with two pairs of related adjectives.

Each pair is:
- followed by a comma
- separated by the conjunction *and*

TEACHING TIPS:

2 pairs sentences are easily grasped by pupils, despite the fact that they invert the syntax that children tend to use.

I find it useful to play the Adjective Pairing Game as a means of introducing the idea. Each pupil in the class is given an adjective written on a piece of paper. They then move around the class until they find another pupil with an adjective that could match theirs. Together they then write a sentence, e.g.

Exhausted and worried, he stumbled away.

PUPILS ONE'S ADJECTIVE   PUPIL TWO'S ADJECTIVE

With their sentence, the pair then moves around the classroom to find pupils who have a second pair of adjectives which can be added to the first pair to create a longer, *2 pairs* sentence, e.g.

Exhausted and worried, cold and hungry, he stumbled away.

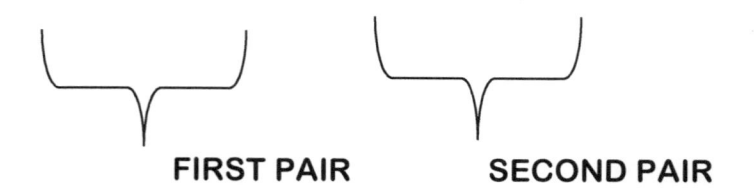

FIRST PAIR   SECOND PAIR

6. TITLE: De : De
OR Description : Details SENTENCES

EXAMPLES:

a. The vampire is a dreadful creature: it kills by sucking all the blood from its victims.

b. Snails are slow: they take hours to cross the shortest of distances.

c. I was exhausted: I hadn't slept for more than two days.

EXPLANATION:

A *Description : Detail* or *De : De* sentence is a compound sentence in which two independent clauses are separated by a colon. The first clause is descriptive and the second adds further details. The colon's function is to signal that the information in the second clause will expand on the information expressed in the first part (before the colon) of the sentence.

TEACHING TIPS:

Once the *De : De* sentence form has been grasped, pupils could be introduced to a variant, in which the first clause of the sentence is an implied question. The easiest way to teach this is : *"It tells the reader something the character is wondering about."*

The clause after the colon then provides the reader with an answer.

e.g.

S/he wondered if it would ever end: it soon would, but not as s/he expected!

(In the example, the second clause is an authorial intrusion—disrupting plot for effect.)

7. TITLE:

Verb, person

SENTENCES

Examples:

a. Flying, John had always been terrified of it.

b. Walking, he seemed to have been walking for ever.

EXPLANATION:

The traditional subject-verb combination is the basis of many sentences. It is possible, however, to invert the typical subject-verb structure and **open** a sentence with a verb in order to give greater importance/weight to that verb. The chosen verb should always be followed with a comma and then the chosen name of a person (or a personal pronoun—he, she, they, it) followed by the remainder of the sentence.

TEACHING TIPS:

This sentence form is particularly powerful when used as a story opening and I have often taught it in this context. If this approach is taken then pupils should be taught that the first verb becomes the main subject of the story. If we take example a. above:

Flying, John had always been terrified of it.

Flying is the opening/operative verb. This would form a perfect opening for a story about a plane crash.

If the teacher wants to develop this, then pupils may be given themes such as:

(i) An earthquake
(ii) An evil ghost

Pupils are then asked to produce *verb, person* sentence story openings for these themes

e.g

(i) Trembling, he had never felt the earth beneath him trembling before ... but this was only the start of it!

(ii) Creeping, John Andrews knew there was something creeping behind him and when he turned and could see nothing, he still knew it was there!

8. TITLE: O. (I.) SENTENCES

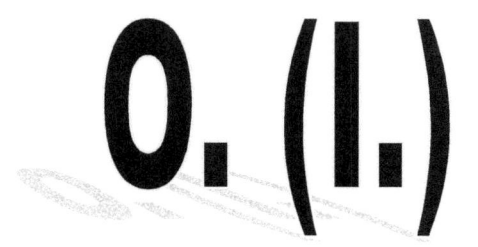

EXAMPLES:

a. He laughed heartily at the joke he had just been told. (At the same time it would be true to say he was quite embarrassed.)

b. She told the little girl not to be so naughty. (Inside, however, she was secretly amused by what she had done.)

c. Jonathan said how pleased he was to be at the party. (It wasn't the truth — he longed to be elsewhere.)

EXPLANATION:

O. (I.) sentences are an abbreviation of Outside:Inside sentences. They are made up of two related sentences. The first tells the reader what a character is supposedly thinking, e.g.

He smiled and shook the man's hand warmly.

This is what is happening on the OUTSIDE, the character's outward actions.

The second, related sentence, which is always placed in brackets, lets the reader know the character's true INNER feelings. Hence:

He smiled and shook the man's hand warmly. (Inside, however, he was more angry than he had ever been.)

The bracketed sentence is also an example of the omniscient, all knowing author. It allows the reader a glimpse of a character's inner thoughts and feelings. It is therefore an authorial intrusion which functions as a disruption of plot for a specific reason—as a hint of future plot development.

TEACHING TIPS:

O. (I.) sentences help pupils to develop more rounded characterisation. I often discuss useful phrases and words which could be used in the second, bracketed sentence:

However ....

In truth .....

Secretly .... etc.

It would also be helpful to discuss the language of opposites, e.g

Happy / sad

Brave / terrified

Calm / angry

Disappointed / elated

9. TITLE: If, if, if, then SENTENCES

EXAMPLES:

a. If the alarm had gone off, if the bus had been on time, if the road repairs had been completed, then his life would not have been destroyed. *

b. If Hannibal hadn't lost, if Rome hadn't won, if Carthage hadn't fallen, then the Mediterranean would be very different today.

c. If I hadn't found that watch, if the alarm hadn't gone off, if it hadn't scared those burglars, then I wouldn't be sitting here today. **

This example would have formed an effective opening to a story if it was followed by a flashback.

**This example demonstrates how the form may be used to end a story by summarising the key/pivotal moments.*

EXPLANATION:

If, if, if, then sentences are constructed from three dependent clauses in series.

Winston Churchill used a similar structure in his speeches, though he often chose three dependent sentences rather than clauses. This speech-writing technique became know as the Churchillian triplet.

The *If, if, if, then* sentence is an extremely useful way of starting or ending a story or idea. It encapsulates a range of themes (which are later developed) in a single sentence. If used to end an idea/story, it acts as a means of summarising the dramatic points of what has gone before.

TEACHING TIPS:

In terms of punctuation, the obvious point to emphasise is the necessity of using a comma after each of the three clauses beginning with *if.*

10. TITLE:

Emotion word , (comma)

SENTENCES

EXAMPLES:

a. Desperate, she screamed for help.

b. Terrified, he froze instantly on the spot where he stood.

c. Anxious, they began to realise that they were lost in the forest.

EXPLANATION:

The *Emotion word (comma)* sentence is a further example of a sentence which does not conform to the traditional subject-verb combination.
It is constructed using an adjective which describes an emotion, followed by a comma. The rest of the sentence describes actions which are related to the opening emotive adjective. Placing the emotive adjective at the start of the sentence gives more weight to that word.

TEACHING TIPS:

As with the *3—Eds* sentences, the use of a poster as a visual learning referent can be very helpful for pupils.

When teaching this sentence form, I produce an A-Z of words which reveal emotions. Pupils are encouraged to add further words to this.....

A	Anxious, Afraid	K	Keen
B	Brave	L	Lucky
C	Cantankerous	M	Maddened
D	Desperate	N	Nostalgic
E	Ecstatic	O	Outraged
F	Fearful	P	Perplexed, Proud
G	Glad	Q	Quietened
H	Happy	R	Ruthless
I	Insolent	S	Sad
J	Joyous	T	Terrified
		U	Unhappy
		V	Vexed
		W	Wearily
		X	
		Y	
		Z	

11. TITLE:

NOUN, which / who / where
SENTENCES

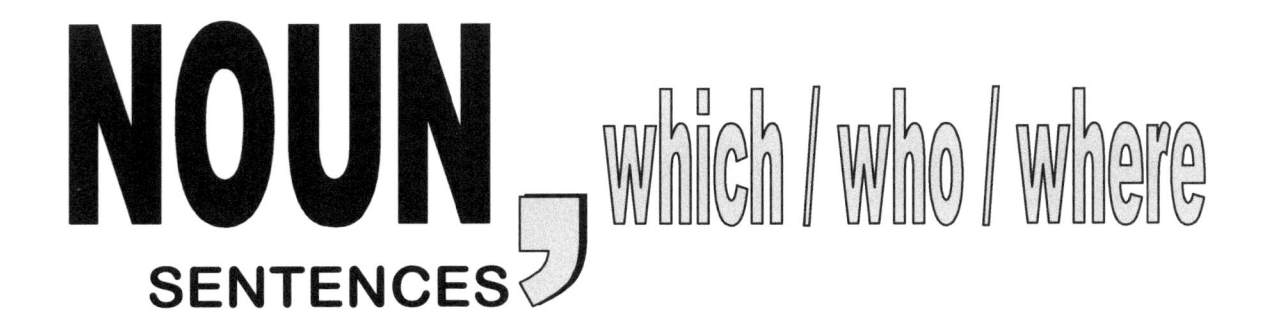

EXAMPLES:

a. Cakes, which taste fantastic, are not so good for your health.

    noun | embedded clause | final part of sentence adding details to noun
    comma   comma

b. Snakes, which scare me, are not always poisonous.

c. My watch, which has to be wound up, works almost as well as one with a battery.

EXPLANATION:

A *Noun, which/who/where* sentence is an example of a sentence with an embedded/ subordinate clause. This sentence always begins with a noun which is followed by a comma then the embedded clause (the part of the sentence that can be omitted and the sentence would still make sense).
The embedded clause ends, as it started, with a comma then the final part of the sentence adds some detail to the opening noun.

TEACHING TIPS:

As sentences with subordinate clauses are difficult to describe to pupils, I find it best to begin with modelled examples. Although a subordinate clause does not always have to begin with the word "which", I find pupils grasp the concept more quickly if they begin writing the subordinate clause with that word.

Once the concept is understood, then more variables can be introduced, e.g.

My mother, <u>who</u> was born in 1944, looks very young for her age.

The garage, <u>where</u> he had his car repaired, has been closed down.

Keep it simple - make it stick!

It should always be remembered that our aim is to make the complex as achievable as possible for the pupils in our classes.
Demonstrating that an embedded clause can be removed and still leave a sentence which makes sense will be familiar to most teachers who have worked on this sentence type with a class. Teachers could use the following game to reinforce this.

Write a selection of starters and endings on the whiteboard, leaving a gap, punctuated with commas, between them.
These should make a sensible sentence on their own.
e.g.

My cat,   , plays with string.

The teacher,   , had taught for a very long time.

The house at the top of the hill,   , had been up for sale for years.

Pupils should then be asked to suggest a middle (the subordinate clause) which, together with the existing start and end, will still make sense. You could then display a selection of middles and ask for starters and endings which work. Points for the most amusing can be awarded!

12. TITLE: MANY QUESTIONS SENTENCE

EXAMPLES:

a. Where is the treasure? the diamonds? the gold? the rubies?

b. What if it rained? it poured? it thundered? it became stormy?

c. How did I feel? yesterday? this morning? now?

EXPLANATION:

This is a useful sentence type to introduce in order to expand punctuation usage beyond full stop and capital letter.

A *Many questions* sentence usually begins with one of the following:

WHO, WHAT, WHERE, WHEN, WHY, HOW or WHAT IF

then an initial question ending with a question mark, followed by further phrases (or even single words) which in themselves pose additional, related questions.

Each of these additional words or phrases is also concluded with a question mark.

TEACHING TIPS:

Although this is a relatively simple sentence type, the most common mistake made by pupils is unnecessary capitalisation. I, therefore, draw attention to the use of a capital letter at the start of the sentence and lower case thereafter.

13. TITLE
Ad, same ad

SENTENCES

EXAMPLES:

a. He was a <u>fast</u> runner, <u>fast</u> because he needed to be.

b. He was a <u>smart</u> dresser, <u>smart</u> because he had the money to buy the best.

c. It was a <u>foolish</u> animal, <u>foolish</u> in a way that will become obvious as this story unfolds.

d. It was a <u>silent</u> town, <u>silent</u> in a way that did not make you feel restful.

EXPLANATION:

An *Ad, same ad* sentence contains two identical adjectives, one repeated shortly after the other.
The first is used in the opening clause of a sentence and the second is used immediately after the comma which ends that clause. This sentence form includes repetition as a way of emphasising an adjective. When used with skill, the repeated word or phrase resonates in the reader's mind.

TEACHING TIPS:

When introducing *Ad, same ad* sentences I always begin by asking pupils to suggest adjectives for a simple sentence in which the adjective has been deliberately omitted.

e.g.

He was a _____ man.

I then model how to turn the pupils' answers into an *Ad, same ad* sentence in the following manner:

1. Add an adjective:

He was a <u>cruel</u> man.

2. Turn the full-stop into a comma :

He was a cruel man,

3. Repeat the adjective after the comma:

He was a cruel man, <u>cruel</u>

4. Add the word *because* after the repeated adjective:

He was a cruel man, cruel <u>because</u>

5. Complete the sentence:

He was a cruel man, cruel, because <u>he always hit his dog.</u>

When pupils have grasped this I model other *Ad, same ad* sentences which use words other than *because* as the bridge to the latter half of the sentence. (Note that examples c and d have used *in a way* as a bridging phrase).

Other words and phrases could be suggested by pupils. Use as a start:

As,

14. TITLE:

3 bad - (dash) question?

SENTENCES

EXAMPLES:

a. Greed, jealousy, hatred — which of these was John Brown's worst trait?

b. Incompetence, arrogance, stupidity — which of these was Custer's fatal flaw?

c. Thirst, heatstroke, exhaustion — which would kill him first?

EXPLANATION:

A *3 bad — (dash) question?* sentence begins with three negative words, the easiest form of which is three negative adjectives. The first and second negative adjectives are followed by commas. The third is followed with a dash, then a question which relates to the negative adjectives. By clustering the negatives, we include a large amount of information in a short, dramatic sentence.

TEACHING TIPS:

A description of this sentence form just ends up being convoluted! It's much easier to give several modelled examples and deconstruct these, accentuating the two commas, dash and question mark which make up the necessary punctuation.

EXTENSION:

A *3 ALTERNATIVES DASH QUESTION?* sentence is a slight variant of the form. Again, this is best taught by examples:

1. Drowning, hanging, shooting — which way would he choose to die?

2. Football, netball, basketball — which sport would be the most popular?

15. TITLE: Double ly ending SENTENCES

EXAMPLES:

a.   He swam slow<u>ly</u> and falter<u>ingly</u>

   ↓   ↘   ↘
   verb   adverb of manner 1   adverb of manner 2

b.   He rode determined<u>ly</u> and swift<u>ly</u>.

c.   He laughed loud<u>ly</u> and hearti<u>ly</u>.

EXPLANATION:

A *Double ly ending* sentence ends with two adverbs of manner. The first part of this sentence type ends in a verb, such as:

   The worried people <u>ran</u>.

This simple sentence is then extended by describing <u>how</u> the people ran, thereby introducing the two adverbs of manner which add precision to the sentence:

   The worried people ran <u>quickly</u> and <u>purposefully.</u>

TEACHING TIPS:

An *A-Z Adverbs of Manner (ly ending words)* poster can be used when focussing on this sentence form. I also model how many adjectives can be turned into adverbs of manner by adding an ly ending:

Quick—quickly
Slow—slowly
Loud—loudly

Once such a list has been produced, we then practise writing sentences with one adverb of manner before introducing the *Double ly* ending type.

When the *Double ly* ending has been mastered, I model how to extend the sentence further by adding an explanatory ending which opens with *because* or *as*. If we take example (a) on the previous page, it could become:

He swam slowly and falteringly <u>because</u> his energy was beginning to ebb away.

16. TITLE: All the W's SENTENCES

EXAMPLES:

a. **Why do you think he ran away?**

(This could be used in the middle of a story as an authorial intrusion in order to maintain the reader's attention. In a sense, it is a cue to read on).

b. **What next?**

(An effective paragraph opening which could be used in the middle of a story after a series of setbacks).

c. **Why is our climate changing?**

(As an opening to arouse interest).

d. **Will that really be the end?**

(As an ending to a story).

EXPLANATION:

All the W's sentences are short sentences which begin with:

>   Who? What? When? Where? Why? Would? Was? Will? What if?

They are used for the following effects:

1. To directly involve the reader.

2. As an opening to a paragraph.

3. As an opening to arouse interest.

4. As an ending to suggest that the reader needs to make up his/her own mind.

TEACHING TIPS:

The main danger with questions, as with alliteration, is that they are scattered too frequently through the writing, thereby losing impact. When to use questions and why we use them? - this should be the central focus of our teaching. Examples which fall into the four categories listed above may be collected and displayed. I also encourage the use of Would? Was? and Will? in addition to the more familiar Who? Where? What? When? When? And Why?

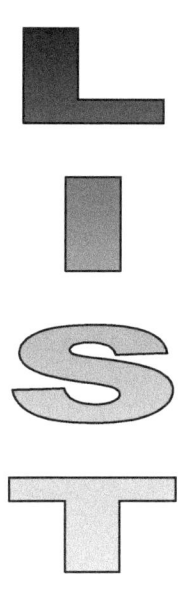

17. TITLE: LIST SENTENCES

EXAMPLES:

a. It was a dark, long, leafy lane.

b. She had a cold, cruel cackle.

c. It was a cold, wet, miserable and misty morning.

EXPLANATION:

A *List* sentence is the most simple sentence form included in this book.

It has no less than three and no more than four adjectives before the noun and, when used judiciously, it creates a striking visual impression in the reader's mind. If combined with alliteration it can also be dramatic in its patterned use of language.

TEACHING TIPS:

In order to introduce list sentences, I show pupils a simple sentence with one word which could obviously be made more powerful. For example:

It was a bad day.

I then underline the word which could be made more powerful (<u>bad</u>) and the pupils suggest alternatives. A typical response is:

wet, cloudy, rainy, dreadful, stormy

I then underline the first letter of each of their suggested words and ask for any other words they could use which begin with these letters. These are used to produce a list:

<u>w</u>	<u>c</u>	<u>r</u>	<u>s</u>	<u>d</u>
wet	cloudy	rainy	stormy	dreadful
windy	cold	rotten	showery	damp
wild				dingy

Finally we combine three or four of these to construct the list sentence:

It was a cold, cloudy, wild and windy day.

N.B. Note the word *and* between the final two adjectives in the list sentence

18. TITLE:

Some; others

SENTENCES

EXAMPLES:

A. Some people love football; others just can't stand it.

(This would be a fantastic introduction to a piece of writing which explored both the merits and failings of football.)

B. Some days are full of enjoyment; others begin and end terribly.

(Used in this way, the *Some; others* sentence forms an effective opening for a story about a day full of terrible events.)

EXPLANATION:

Some; others sentences are, as suggested in the name, compound sentences which begin with the word *some* and have a semi-colon rather than a conjunction which separates the latter half of the sentence. They are useful as a way of introducing a dilemma/argument in both fiction and non-fiction contexts.

TEACHING TIPS:

It is sometimes useful to demonstrate how the semi-colon replaces the word *but*. Actively crossing out the word *but* and replacing it with a semi-colon can help pupils to place the semi-colon correctly. I also stress that the word following the semi-colon should n<u>ot</u> be capiltalised, as numerous pupils I have taught have fallen into this habit.

19. TITLE:
Personification of weather

SENTENCES

EXAMPLES:

a. The rain <u>wept</u> down the window = sad mood

b. The wind <u>screamed</u> through the branches = tense mood

c. The breeze <u>murmured</u> through the branches = happy mood

d. The snow <u>smothered</u> the town = tense, claustrophobic mood

EXPLANATION:

To produce one of these sentences, an element of the weather, such as rain or wind, is given a human attribute.

If the *rain wept*, then the word *wept* is the human attribute which personifies the weather. This sentence is particularly useful for creating mood in a story. The *rain weeping*, for example, creates a sad mood.

TEACHING TIPS:

To ascertain whether pupils are ready for *Personification of weather* sentences, I play personification games in which we 'bring to life' objects in the classroom.

Sometimes we make a pencil or pen talk using the following sentence starters:

1.   I like ……………………………………………………………

2. I don't like …………………………………………………

3. I'm happy when …………………………………………

4. I'm sad when ……………………………………………

5. I'd rather be ………………………………………………

If the responses are too short, add the word *because* to the end of each!

When pupils have demonstrated their ability to personify using this method, then we begin to personify the weather.

I use a range of strategies to embed understanding of this sentence type including:

- underlining the *personified* word in given examples

- adding a *personified word* in sentences with these omitted

- linking sounds and actions which humans make and do when they are happy, sad, angry, frightened etc.

EXTENSION ACTIVITY:

Ask pupils to add adverbs of manner to the simple personification sentences:

The rain wept down the window.

might become:

The rain wept <u>pitifully</u> down the window.

20. TITLE: P.C. SENTENCES

EXAMPLES:

a. It was <u>both</u> cold <u>and</u> unpleasant for him to work there.

b. It was <u>not so</u> much lack of time <u>as</u> fear that stopped him from taking the job.

c. <u>Neither</u> money <u>nor</u> gifts could make him visit the haunted mansion again.

d. He was <u>as</u> silly <u>as</u> a clown.

EXPLANATION:

P.C. is a shortened version of *Paired Conjunctions* (sometimes referred to as correlative conjunctions).

Some words demand a second word in order to make sense—this is the essence of a paired conjunction.

TEACHING TIPS:

A useful mnemonic which helps pupils to remember some of the paired conjunctions is:

(B A) (N A) (N N) (A A)

(note the double NN and AA at the end)

This stands for:

(B A) - both/and
(N A) - not so/as
(NN) - neither/nor
(AA) - as/as

I tend to add *whether...or* to the (B A) (N A) (N N) (AA) paired conjunctions and, of course, there are others such as *so/that* which may be added if the teacher wishes.

21. TITLE: *The more, the more*

SENTENCES

EXAMPLES:

a. The <u>more</u> upset she was, the <u>more</u> her tears flowed.
          emotion   comma   action related to emotion

b. The <u>more</u> happy she became, the <u>more</u> talkative she seemed to be.
          emotion   comma   action related to emotion

c. The <u>more</u> angry he became, the <u>more</u> he hammered his fist on the table.
          emotion   comma   action related to emotion

EXPLANATION:

As with sentence type 20, *The more, the more* sentence is a paired form, particularly useful when developing a character trait in a story. The first *more* should be followed by an emotive word and the second *more* should be followed by a related action.

TEACHING TIPS:

I begin by producing a list of human emotions with the pupils. I then model a *The more, the more* sentence based on one of these. The pupils, in pairs, then produce their own sentences from the remaining emotions.

EXTENSION:

A useful extension is *The less, the less* sentence, e.g.

The <u>less</u> happy he became, the <u>less</u> likely he was to smile.

It is also possible to produce *The more, the less* sentences and *The less, the more* variants.

All in all, this is an extremely useful sentence type when developing characters within a story.

22. TITLE: SHORT SENTENCES

EXAMPLES:

a. Then it happened.

b. Everything failed.

c. Oh no!

d. Stop ... s ... stop!

EXPLANATION:

Short sentences are formed with one, two or three words. Many one word sentences are, in fact, interjections which demand an exclamation mark: (necessary when the single word is uttered when shocked, surprised, angry, upset worried etc.).
e.g.

> Ouch! Help! Ugh!

One, two or three word sentences are only useful if they are used in the following contexts:

1. After several long sentences (for dramatic effect)

2. As a way of developing tension within the plot: *That wasn't all.*

3. As an authorial intrusion: *It's true.*

4. In speech, between characters, to indicate tension:

"Up there."
"Where?"
"At the window."
"What?"
"A gun!"

TEACHING TIPS:

Focus on modelling this sentence type in context. If taught effectively, there will be much discussion of the writing which precedes and the writing which follows the short sentence (or sentences). In narrative it is useful to link short sentences and dilemma.

Although they should not be overused, ellipsis marks (three full stops in a row) can be used to indicate a stutter, itself indicative of fear. (See example d. on previous page.)

23. TITLE:

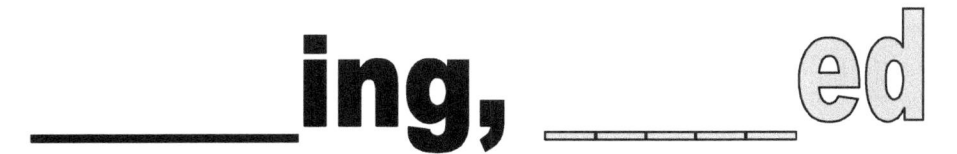

_____ing, _____ed

SENTENCES

EXAMPLES:

a. Walk<u>ing</u> in the bush, she stopp<u>ed</u> at the sight of a crocodile facing her.

b. Runn<u>ing</u> near the beach, he halt<u>ed</u> as the ground gave way.

EXPLANATION:

An ____*ing*, ____*ed* sentence always begins with a verb ending in *ing* followed by the location of the action and then a comma:

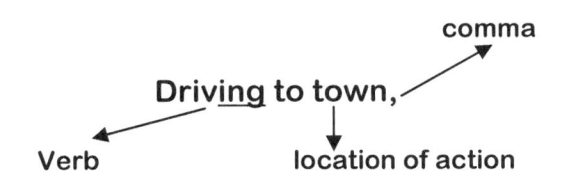

Driv*ing* to town,
- Verb
- location of action
- comma

After this comma, the latter part of the sentence begins with a name or personal pronoun followed by a second verb with an *ed* ending and a pivotal incident:

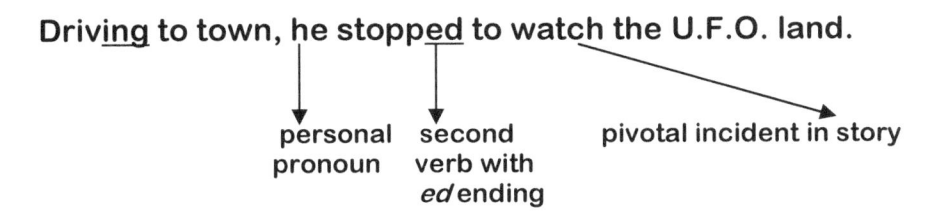

Driv*ing* to town, he stopp*ed* to watch the U.F.O. land.
- personal pronoun
- second verb with *ed* ending
- pivotal incident in story

The sentence form adds variety as it inverts the typical subject/verb form and moves from present to past tense. It is particularly useful in a story when something dramatic occurs which will affect the plot.

TEACHING TIPS:

I always begin by listing as many verbs as possible with the present tense ending (_ing). The pupils are then paired up. One produces the first part of the sentence and the other completes it. After a given amount of time (usually 10—15 minutes) I ask the pupils to swap roles so that the pupil who has previously written the opening part of the sentence now produces the conclusion.

24. TITLE: Irony

SENTENCES

EXAMPLES:

a. Our 'luxury' hotel turned out to be a farm outbuilding.

b. The 'trip of our dreams' was, in fact, our worst nightmare.

c. With dawn breaking the 'beautiful view', which the brochure described, revealed itself to be a scrap-yard and rubbish tip.

EXPLANATION:

An Irony sentence deliberately overstates how good or bad something is.

The overstated word such as *wonderful* or *terrible* is then shown to be a falsehood in the remainder of the sentence, when truth is evidenced. (as in the examples above.)

TEACHING TIPS:

It is useful to begin by discussing and collecting superlatives which can be used in the initial, ironic, part of the sentence. Once again, an A-Z of superlatives can form a useful visual element of class display:

A	Amazing, astounding	I	Incredible	Q	
B	Best	J		R	
C	Colossal	K		S	Superb
D	Delicious	L		T	Tremendous
E	Exciting	M	Marvellous	U	Unbeatable
F	Fantastic	N		V	Value-for-money
G	Great	O		W	Wonderful
H	Horrendous	P	Perfect		

25. TITLE
IMAGINE 3 examples:

SENTENCES

EXAMPLES:

a. Imagine a time when people were not afraid, when life was much simpler, when everyone helped each other: this is the story of that time.

b. Imagine a place where the sun always shines, where wars never happen, where no-one ever dies: in the Andromeda 5 system, there is such a planet.

EXPLANATION:

Imagine three examples: sentences begin with the word Imagine, and then describe three facets of something (often times or places). The first two facets are separated by commas and the third concludes with a colon. The writer then explains that such a time or place exists.

This is a superb sentence type to use at the start of a science fiction or fantasy story.

TEACHING TIPS:

Once the sentence type has been modelled and discussed I ask pupils to write *Imagine three examples:* sentences for the following:

1. A perfect planet.

2. A week when everything goes wrong.

3. The best Christmas day ever.

4. A wonderful holiday.

5. A dreadful battle in a war.

If pupils find this difficult, more modelling and discussion needs to take place.

APPENDIX 1
COLOUR CODED DISPLAY AND TARGET SETTING

In order to link class display and target setting, a 'Sentences Poster' can be produced with several (or all) of the sentence types included. Each should be written in a different colour:

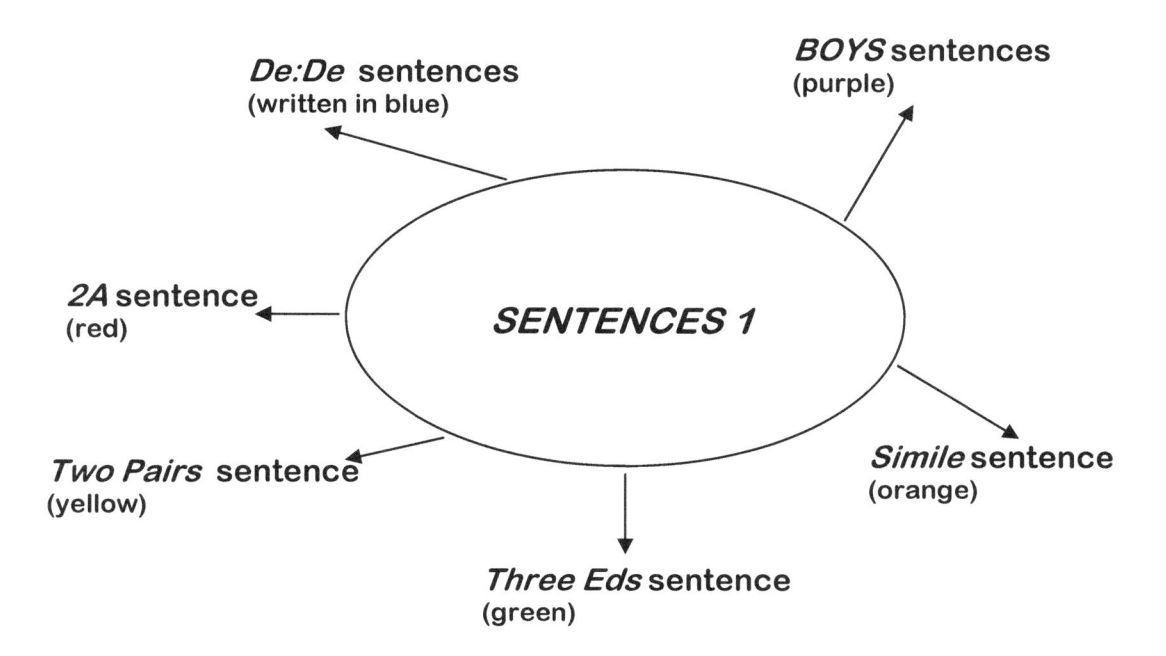

```
        De:De sentences              BOYS sentences
        (written in blue)            (purple)
                    ↖        ↗
    2A sentence  ←  ( SENTENCES 1 )
    (red)                            →  Simile sentence
                    ↙        ↓          (orange)
    Two Pairs sentence
    (yellow)        Three Eds sentence
                    (green)
```

To differentiate, several of these could be produced so that one group of pupils could be directed to the *SENTENCES 1* poster while a second group could be directed to the *SENTENCES 2* poster which may have more complex sentence types.

In order to link this display to target setting, pupils need access to either coloured pencils, pens or highlighters which match the colours used on the posters.

Pupils can then be asked (for example) to *include two red sentences, one orange sentence and a blue sentence* in their writing.

For the teacher the main advantage of this approach is more efficient marking. Colour coded sentences stand out from the main body of the text and therefore it is easier to ascertain if a pupil has met their target of using a broad range of sentence types.

The advantage for pupils is that the teacher can spend time, previously expended in searching for achievements, in acknowledging them.

Colour coded display, linked to target setting and a school's marking policy, is an efficient way of sharpening the focus of either fiction or non-fiction writing.

APPENDIX 2
USING A BROAD RANGE OF CONNECTIVES:
THE PHYSICAL REMINDERS POSTER

The ability to use a broad range of connectives is useful in many of the sentence types included in this book.

One invaluable addition to the teacher's repertoire for developing pupil understanding of connectives is a *Physical Reminder* poster. The one I use is included below:

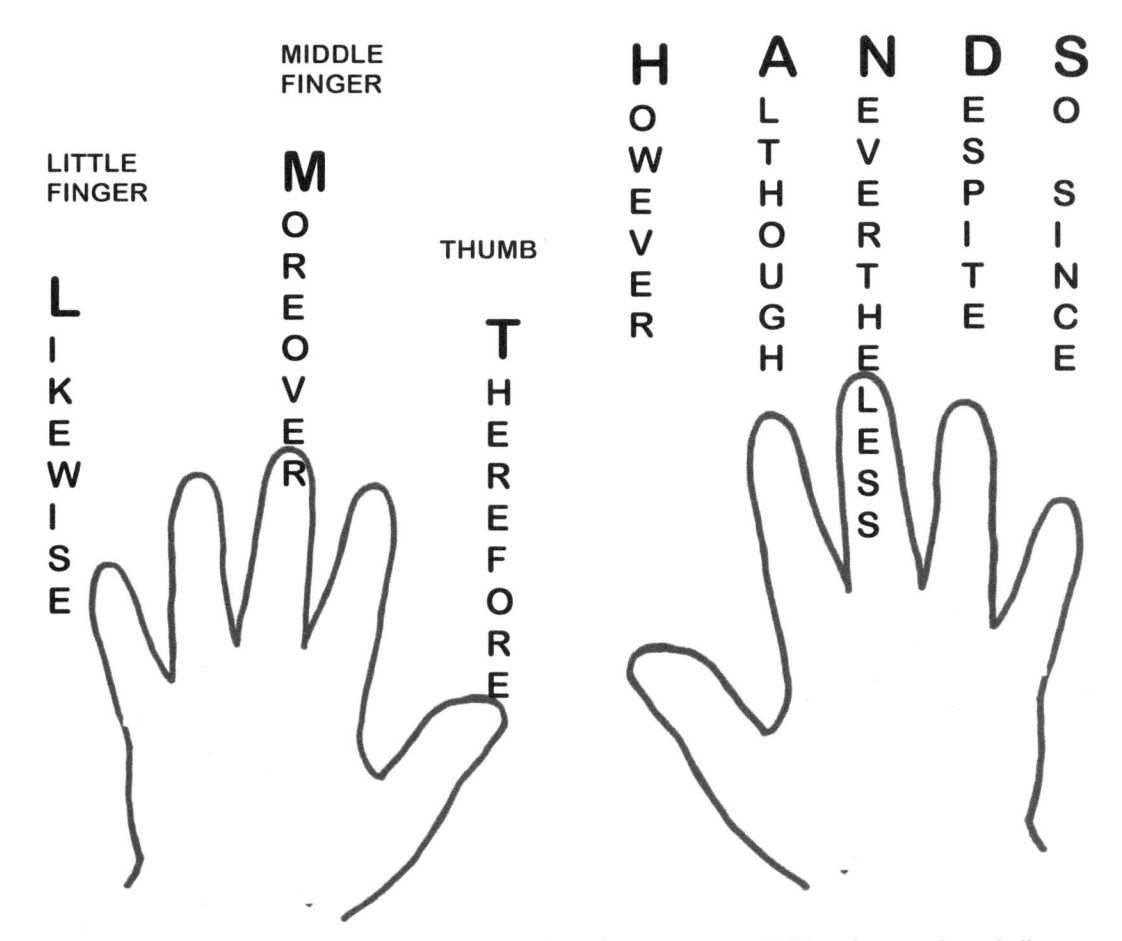

MIDDLE FINGER

LITTLE FINGER

THUMB

Left hand fingers (little to thumb): **LIKEWISE**, **MOREOVER**, **THEREFORE**

Right hand (thumb to little finger): **HANDS** — **HOWEVER**, **ALTHOUGH**, **NEVERTHELESS**, **DESPITE**, **SO SINCE**

When pupils complete a piece of writing the teacher can say: "*Check your hands.*"

Their hands then function as a physical (kinaesthetic) reminder of a broad range of connectives—specifically:

However, Although, Nevertheless, Despite, So, Since, Therefore, Moreover, Likewise

Clearly pupils should not be taught that they must use all of these connectives in each piece of writing. Their hands merely act as a reminder of a range of connectives

One school I worked with also produced this as a poster titled *Handy Connectives*, another adapted the idea of *Physical Reminders* for younger children. They pointed to their ABS (abdominal muscles) as a physical reminder of And, But and So.

APPENDIX 3

***Writing Exciting Sentences* was trialled in a number of schools across the UK.**

Jon Westwood, Year 6 teacher at Wyche Primary School, Malvern, Worcestershire provided his thoughts on the concept, effectiveness and outcomes of the project.

The following are examples of sentences taken from my pupils' narrative writing since I introduced the idea of including different sentence types.

2A Sentences

These had been taught incorrectly throughout the school, no child could successfully explain or describe what a 2A sentence was. After using the book:

EXAMPLES FROM PUPILS

The huge, green tractor ploughed the muddy, wet field. (Kimberley Palmer)
The newsreader was a tall, dark man with an old, leather jacket. (Hope Speight)
The glistening, soft snow, twinkling in the pitch black night faded away. (Tim Tedds)

3_ed Sentences

The kids have loved these, no problems using them, they just needed to be highlighted, job done!

EXAMPLES FROM PUPILS

Confused, excited, frightened I quickly drove away. (Katie Jackson-Read)
Petrified, frightened, horrified I glared at the door.
Delighted, astonished, bewildered he couldn't believe what he saw in front of him. (Alice Kent)
Scared, confused, betrayed I slumped to the floor. (Ed Lowe)
Horrified, petrified, scared I ran out of the door and pushed my way through the crowd of scared people. (Hope Speight)

2 pairs sentences

As above, simple. Easy to use, even easier to teach!

EXAMPLES FROM PUPILS

Tired and lonely, cold and hungry, he continued to stack the hay. (Hope Speight)
Lost and confused, dazed and thirsty, the fox searched for his den. (Alice Kent)
Tired and lonely, cold and hungry, I was beginning to add the mixture into the rocket.

Verb, person

Kids have struggled with these sentences. Not sure why, but they haven't used them as frequently as some of the others.

EXAMPLES FROM PUPILS

>Punching, John was winning his battle against the bully. (Cameron Lewis)
>Crying, Fred convinced his mum it wasn't his fault. (Harry Senior)
>Startled, I shot out from under my dodo feathered duvet and grabbed my clothes. (Harry Davies)
>Terrified, we dived into a nearby hallway guns blasting. (Harry Senior)

O.(I). Sentences

We've been doing these for a while now, kids are happy with these.

EXAMPLES FROM PUPILS

>Steve MaClaren smiled and shook the hand of the Croatian coach but he resented the fact that England were out of the Euro Championships. *Thought you might like this one, one of my boys came in and modelled this one. It made me laugh!* (Combination of boys)
>She laughed at the comment made about her hair however it deeply offended her. (Kimberley Palmer)
>I was delighted. (But I felt scared something was about to go wrong) (Josh Brooks)
>Bravely I looked behind me. (But I was deeply worried) (Bethany Williams)

If, if,if, then

A new one to them, no-one familiar with this type of sentence, but pupils of all abilities have grasped it very well.

EXAMPLES FROM PUPILS

>If Charlie had walked, if he had wiped his feet, if he had stayed with his partner, then they would have won the orienteering competition. (Jonah Pickering)
>If only we could find some way to fix it, if only we had brought some tools from Earth, if only I'd brought someone with me, then it would have been so much easier. (Marcello Cossali-Francis)
>If Bertie had been more careful, if he had listened to his teacher, if he had walked when crossing the road, then he would still be with us today. (Jonah Pickering)

Extended Simile

My favourite! Been doing this for a while. The kids are having so much fun with these and I've been really impressed with them. They are so easy to create and have huge impact on writing.

EXAMPLES FROM PUPILS

The water rushed past like a herd of buffalos evading a predator.
The light was as bright as the moon shining on a cloudless night in the middle of December. (Dan Sillitoe)
I looked up at the moon. It was as bright as brand new lights dangling from a glossy, sparkly, frosted, artificial Christmas tree.
The ship floated past Mercury like a feather falling from a bird on a warm, clear summer day. (Jonah Pickering)
Looking out of the window I saw the Earth like a tiny plastic model that children have in schools floating around the blackness of space. (Gillian Wright)
Thoughts struck me like a blaze of thunder an a dark stormy night. (Matty Chauhan)
Passengers were screaming so loud it was like a chicken about to have his head chopped off. (Harry Davies)

3 Question openers?

What about a fourth question? A year 6 pupil did this:

Have you ever wondered what life would be like in the year 3003? Have you ever imagined what it would be like if robots ruled the Earth? Or have you ever imagined what it would be like on a space station? Have you? (Harry Senior)

EXAMPLES FROM PUPILS

I was on the spot! Should I help NASA? Should I risk my life for other people? Should I help the Earth? (Marcello Cossali-Francis)
Have you ever seen an alien? Have you ever experienced extra terrestrial travel? Have you ever been into space? Well I have and this is my story. (William Waite)

An interesting point to note: I started using such sentences in my marking to model them to the kids.

e.g. "If only you had put full stops in, if only you had varied your sentence beginning, if only you had used 2A sentences then the story would have been more exciting."

This is very critical. It highlights targets for them next time. My classroom operates on a very honest basis. The kids tell me if the lessons are boring! It works both ways, so this way of marking works for me.

Emotion word, comma

We kind of do these naturally throughout the school, very easy to teach, though it is through chance rather than strategic planning!

EXAMPLES FROM PUPILS

Terrified, he knew he may never communicate with Earth again.
Happily, the astronaut stepped safely from the space shuttle. (Hope Speight)

Ad, same ad

Not taught these before, love them. Kids again had a ball with them.

> He was an aggressive man, aggressive in a way that really scared me.
> The hills were misty, misty because rain had just settled.
> They were weird, weird in a way that really freaked me out. (Sally Fitzpatrick)

3 bad – (dash)

We decided that this was one of the most powerful sentences. A lot of detail within a short sentence really improved characterisation.

EXAMPLES FROM PUPILS

> Trapped, alone, destroyed—how would I ever get to the space station? (Kimberley Palmer)
> Dark, lifeless, cold – what would we do without the moon? (Dan Sillitoe)
> Heartbroken, cold, blank faced – was that really the end? Surely not?
> (Marcello Cossali-Francis.)
> Hungry, thirsty, angry – would I die here? (Harry Senior)

Double ly ending

Very easy to use! Very easy to teach!

Some;others

Just got on to these, excellent to teach purposeful use of semi-colon.

P.C. Sentences

Haven't done much work with these to be honest.

The more, the more sentences

Used to enhance characterisation

Irony sentences

Been doing these for a while to introduce inverted commas and sarcasm.

Sentence types we have already been teaching:

Personification, List, Short

POINTS OF INTEREST ALONG THE WAY

*Whole school integration! These sentence types have been so rewarding to use within the classroom, not only for myself but for the children to use to improve their work. It was fascinating to watch.
The children simply came alive trying to impress me with their exciting sentences.
For example, in RE we were looking at the formation of the khalsa – a celebration linked to Sikhism. The children used several sentence types to re-write, in their own words, how it all came about! Brilliant!*
HOWEVER my job would have been made much easier if the children had experienced these sentence types earlier in school. Having used the sentence types, some we thought were quite difficult haven't been so difficult to teach! So our progression grid will be amended accordingly. It's so important that these sentences are happening across or throughout the whole school.

SEN
Our SEN support teacher got wind of what we were doing and requested a copy of the sentence types. She got so excited on two accounts:
> *1. Some of the sentences she was teaching already but many examples she had never heard of and is now using them with her SEN group.*
> *2. She then went home and taught them to her son who is at secondary school. He thrived on them!*

MARKING AND MODELLING

*I know this is taking it a little too far but I modelled the sentence types within my own marking.
e.g. "If only you had put a comma in, if only you had used speech marks, if only you had put capitals for proper nouns then I would have been so much happier!"
This is sad and was a little corny but it did work! Just a thought!*

Display

All the different sentence types should be displayed in the classroom. Mine are all abbreviated and placed around my clock—the place kids and teachers look towards the most! I simply ask them, when proof reading, to put in a 3 bad-dash question sentence. AND THEY DO!

Punctuation

It gets the kids using a wide range of punctuation marks effectively!

TO SUM UP…

When I first looked at the sentences I did assume that some of them would be beyond even Year 6, but after teaching them, I beg to differ. They work at all levels. When my underachieving kids are putting Extended Similes and Ad, same ad sentences into their work and punctuating correctly that's a job done!

Fantastic, I loved teaching them, to be honest it will change my teaching dramatically.
This isn't lip service, it truly will change how I teach the putting together of sentences to good effect in both fiction and non-fiction writing. Half of these sentences I'd never taught, but the scariest thing for me is that many, many kids will never see these sentences, and that's a crime!

Thanks again.

Jon Westwood

ALSO AVAILABLE FROM
CREATIVE EDUCATIONAL PRESS
WWW.THECEPRESS.COM

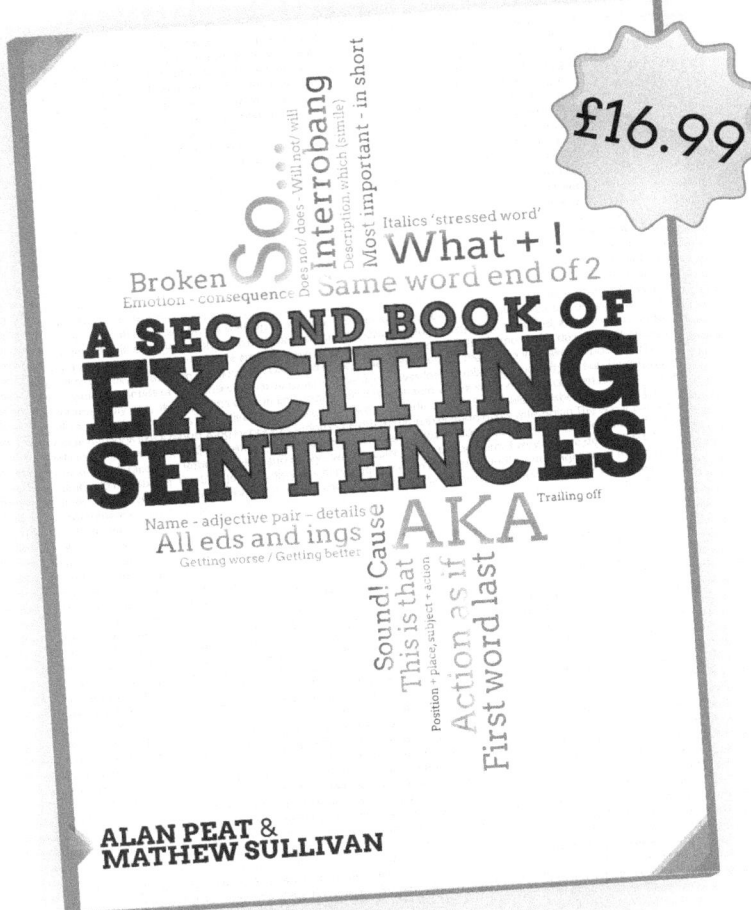

A SECOND BOOK OF EXCITING SENTENCES

£16.99

30 Brand new sentence types! This time with direct links to both fiction and non-fiction genres. Written by Alan Peat and Mathew Sullivan, this timely book is filled with practical ideas.

DEVELOPING WRITING THROUGH COMICS

£19.99

THE BOOK WILL:

Demonstrate how comics and hybrid texts can be used to engage reluctant readers and improve comprehension skills at all levels.

Show how comics can be used to aid narrative planning.

Enable teachers to use comic heroes, as well as other fictional and non fictional figures, to develop character writing.

Provide ways of using comics to enhance locational descriptions.

Suggest ways to use comics to make the teaching of spelling, punctuation and grammar exciting and memorable.

Give gifted and talented pupils ways to access higher level ideas through comics.

EFFECTIVE SCHOOL BASED TRAINING FOR ALL STAFF

Alan runs school-based training on Literacy and Thinking Skills

Prices start at **£975 + VAT** (plus **£85** towards local accommodation, the night prior to the event, plus 'at cost' travelling expenses) for a single school.

For **two** schools clustering the price drops to **£750** per school and for **three** schools to **£675** per school.

For larger numbers fees are negotiated directly with Alan.

IF SCHOOLS WISH TO SELL OUT ADDITIONAL PLACES TO OFFSET COSTS WE ASK THAT THEY CHARGE NO MORE THAN £95 PER PLACE. We add an additional £55 for each place 'sold on' and the school retains £40.

To book a place either call

07789938923

or email

info@alanpeat.com

Visit www.alanpeat.com for further information

Teaching Outstanding Persuasive Writing (with 7-16 year olds) is a must-have for the busy teacher. Packed full of tried-and-tested, effective strategies, the book provides:

- Structural models that really work!
- Eleven easy-to-teach opening strategies
- Nineteen high-impact language techniques
- Four clearly described endings
- Seven photocopiable language –support sheets for pupils
- Samples of work from the trial group
- A wealth of brand new ideas, guaranteed to enrich both teachers' and pupils' understanding of persuasive writing.

£17.99

To order your copy visit: www.alanpeat.com and use the request form on the contact page.

Using the XBOX 360 as a Stimulus for Literacy

By Russell Newman
With an introduction by Alan Peat

Age 7-14

£19.99

In this exciting new book, Russell Newman provides busy teachers with a wealth of practical, engaging ideas which are guaranteed to motivate and inspire pupils to write. All activities included in this book use, as a starting point, the XBOX 360 console and a range of easily downloaded demos.

Computers and video games are one of the most effective ways to 'reach' reluctant writers and this is certainly a book which will prove to be a valuable tool in the drive to raise both fiction and non-fiction writing standards!

"Writing is a stubborn problem in many of our schools and doing more of what we are already doing (in such a context) is unlikely to alter this situation."
Alan Peat

Don't miss THIS BRAND NEW TITLE FROM Creative Educational Press Ltd.

To order your copy visit: www.alanpeat.com and use the request form on the contact page.